The Voice of the Martyrs is a Christian nonprofit ministry dedicated to serving Christians who are persecuted for their faith. The ministry helps Christians living in nations hostile to the gospel, including communist and Islamic countries. Founded in 1967 by Richard and Sabina Wurmbrand, a Romanian couple once imprisoned for their faith, The Voice of the Martyrs has a network of offices around the globe dedicated to helping the persecuted church. The ministry fulfills the Wurmbrands' vision to raise awareness about the plight of the persecuted church and to assist those suffering for their Christian witness.

To receive a free newsletter and learn how you can help today's persecuted church, contact:

The Voice of the Martyrs
PO Box 443
Bartlesville, OK 74005
(800) 747-0085
E-mail: thevoice@vom-usa.org
Website: www.persecution.com
Youth website: www.kidsofcourage.com

For Ainsley and Chaney.
May the generous and tenacious faith of Nicholas
inspire you to stand for Jesus…
no matter what!
Love, Mom

For our persecuted brethren,
who, like Nicholas,
dare to stand up for Jesus,
risking imprisonment and death.

A Note to Parents and Educators

Throughout history many legends about the life of Saint Nicholas (of Myra) have circulated around the world, bringing us to whom we know today as Santa Claus—a man in a red suit who with his reindeer delivers presents to good boys and girls on Christmas Eve.

But who is this man behind the myth of Santa Claus?

Nicholas of Myra was born in the third century in a province called Lycia, which was a part of the Roman Empire. Today ancient Lycia is a part of the country we know as Turkey. Nicholas is believed to have died around A.D. 343, on December 6th, a date that is celebrated today by many nations, such as Germany, Switzerland, and the Netherlands, and is called "Saint Nicholas Day." For example, in Germany, children are known to put a boot, called a Nikolaus-Stiefel, outside their front door on the eve of Saint Nicholas Day, hoping he will fill it with gifts if he thinks they were good. But if found bad, they will receive a lump of charcoal.

Tradition tells us that the real Nicholas was a man full of generosity and conviction. He was born to wealthy parents who left him their fortune when they died. Instead of squandering his inheritance on himself, he used it to help those in need. For example, one of the stories in the book shares about three sisters who were saved from life on the streets. Because their father did not have enough money for their dowries, he was unable to arrange suitable marriages and was left with no other choice but to sell them to a brothel. (In the story, I refer to this tragedy as "life on the streets.") Upon hearing this, Nicholas secretly threw bags of gold into the girls' room. The father was elated. After discovering his daughters' mysterious benefactor, the father was sworn to secrecy.

Tradition also says that Nicholas is known to have exposed a corrupt government official who hoarded grain until the demand pushed it to a higher price. And later, Nicholas intervened in an execution of three innocent men—all falsely accused by the same crooked governor. It is said that one of the prisoners was situated on the block for decapitation, and Nicholas grabbed the sword from the executioner's hands, setting all three free. He was praised for his bravery.

Even though many have preserved the stories of Nicholas' righteous acts, few know of his sufferings for Christ. Sometime after the Roman emperor Diocletian took power (ruled from A.D. 284 – 305), he instigated a horrific persecution of Christians. Nicholas was imprisoned and physically tortured (one source says pinched with hot iron pliers) for refusing to deny Jesus as God. According to Eusebius' *The Church History*, an imperial edict was issued, ordering that church leaders all over the empire be arrested and imprisoned. Eusebius writes that prisons were so full of church leaders and workers that there was no room for the actual criminals. Diocletian destroyed churches and confiscated and burned

Scriptures. The killing of Christians became a form of entertainment for the Romans. The year A.D. 303 was when Diocletian aimed to finish off the church for good. However, he failed. The courage of believers who were martyred for their witness had caused many others to place their faith in Jesus Christ. Having failed, Diocletian abdicated the throne in A.D. 305. According to one source, he returned home to be a cabbage farmer. From the time of Nero to A.D. 313, some estimate that 3 million Christians were martyred.

After the reign of persecution ended, Nicholas would still face a fierce testing of his faith, this time within the church. A preacher named Arius began promoting a heresy that questioned the Deity of Jesus Christ. Arius' false teachings (which would be called Arianism) were even set to music by putting words to popular drinking songs. Constantine, the new leader of the Roman Empire, called together church leaders at Nicea to discuss Arius' teachings, among other issues. This was the Council of Nicea. According to legend, as Arius was making his presentation, he began singing one of his blasphemous songs about Jesus. Unwilling to see this man shame Christ, Nicholas stood up and punched Arius in the mouth. Those in attendance were shocked! Although they understood Nicholas' need to stand up for Christ's reputation, they did not believe they could allow such behavior since Christ taught us to love our enemies and live a life of peace. Therefore, Nicholas was no longer allowed to serve as bishop. (Some say that he was later restored to his position.) But this action did not stop Nicholas from serving the sick and helping the needy. It's important to note that some have questioned Nicholas' presence at the Council of Nicea because his name is not listed on the Council roster.

The persecution of Christians is not confined to Nicholas' time in history. Those who have chosen to witness for Christ have been persecuted. Even today Christians are being persecuted in communist and Islamic nations for knowing Jesus Christ and telling others about Him. In communist countries, meeting for a Bible study in a home is considered illegal and owning a Bible could sentence a person to several years in prison. In Islamic nations, Muslims who convert to Christianity have been rejected by family members and even gunned down on the street by jihadist Muslims.

Many who are persecuted for following Christ today are much like Nicholas of Myra: They humbly serve their fellow countrymen and courageously stand for the Lord when faced with the choice of prison with Christ or no prison without Christ. His story of boldness and generosity in the face of persecution from the government and conflict within the church is for anyone. By any Christian definition, Nicholas was indeed a saint.

May Nicholas' life challenge us to live generously by serving the poor and courageously by standing for Christ in a culture that is increasingly hostile to Him and His people!

"Let's name him Nicholas."

1

About 200 years after the birth of Jesus, a boy was born to wealthy parents in a land called Lycia.

"Let's name him Nicholas," they said, and they loved him with all their hearts.

But when Nicholas was still very young, his parents died, leaving him all of their money.

"I will use this to help the poor," Nicholas decided. And so began his life of giving to those in need.

3

"I will use this to help the poor."

4

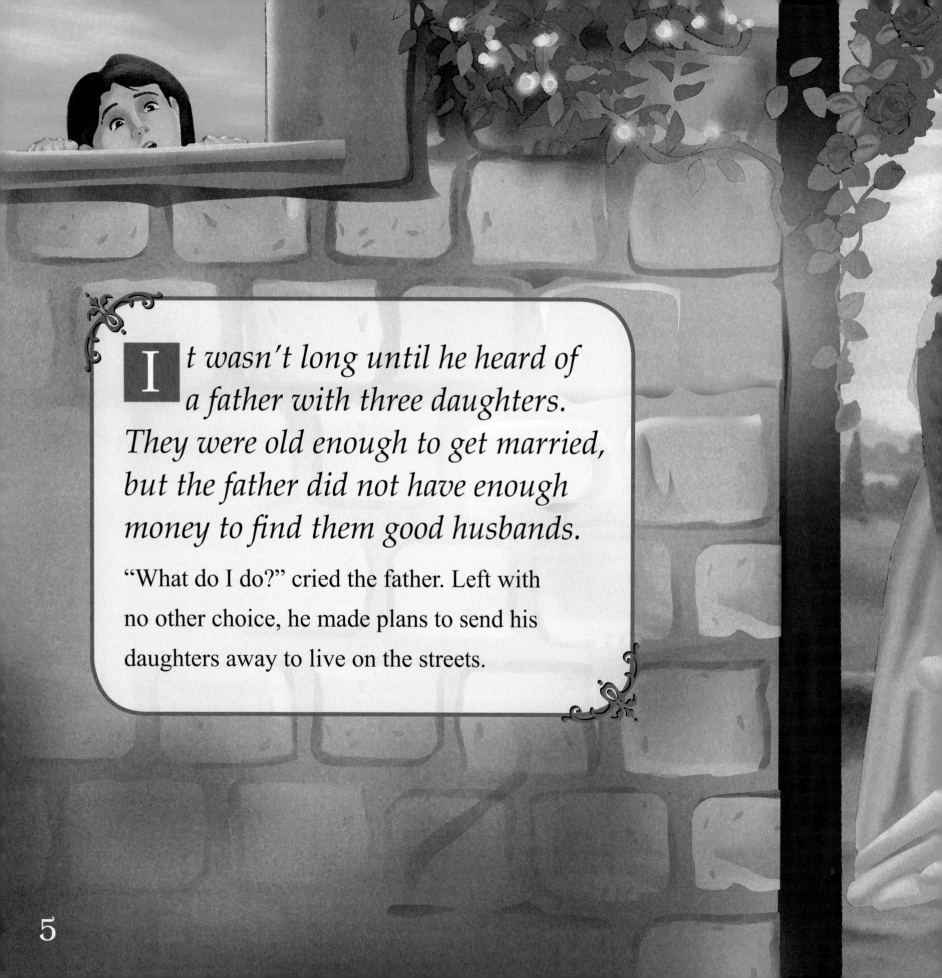

It wasn't long until he heard of a father with three daughters. They were old enough to get married, but the father did not have enough money to find them good husbands.

"What do I do?" cried the father. Left with no other choice, he made plans to send his daughters away to live on the streets.

"What do I do?

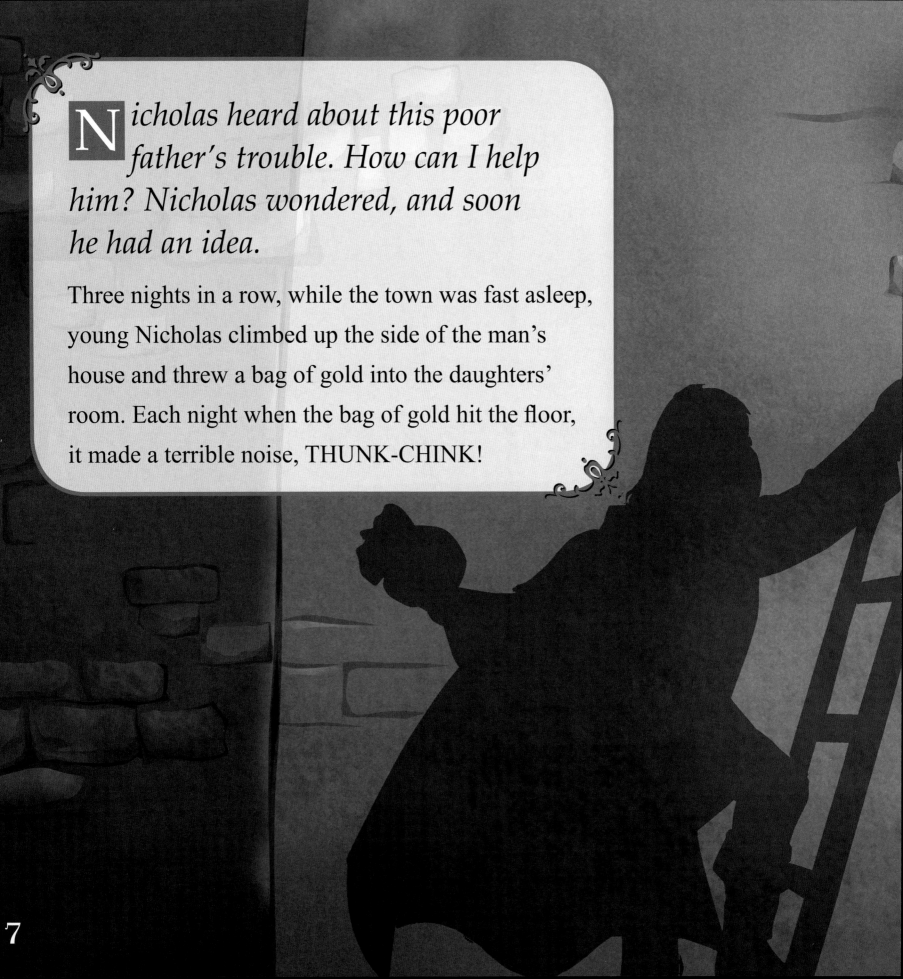

N icholas heard about this poor
father's trouble. How can I help
him? Nicholas wondered, and soon
he had an idea.

Three nights in a row, while the town was fast asleep,
young Nicholas climbed up the side of the man's
house and threw a bag of gold into the daughters'
room. Each night when the bag of gold hit the floor,
it made a terrible noise, THUNK-CHINK!

"You cannot tell anyone what I have done for you!"

E very night this noise would wake up the father and his daughters, so on the third night the father stayed awake to meet this secret giver.

As soon as the father heard the THUNK-CHINK! he grabbed the mysterious person and discovered hc was just a young man.

"You cannot tell anyone what I have done for you!" Nicholas pleaded quietly.

The father promised he would never say a word. He sang for joy that Nicholas had saved his daughters from a life on the streets, and now he could find them good husbands.

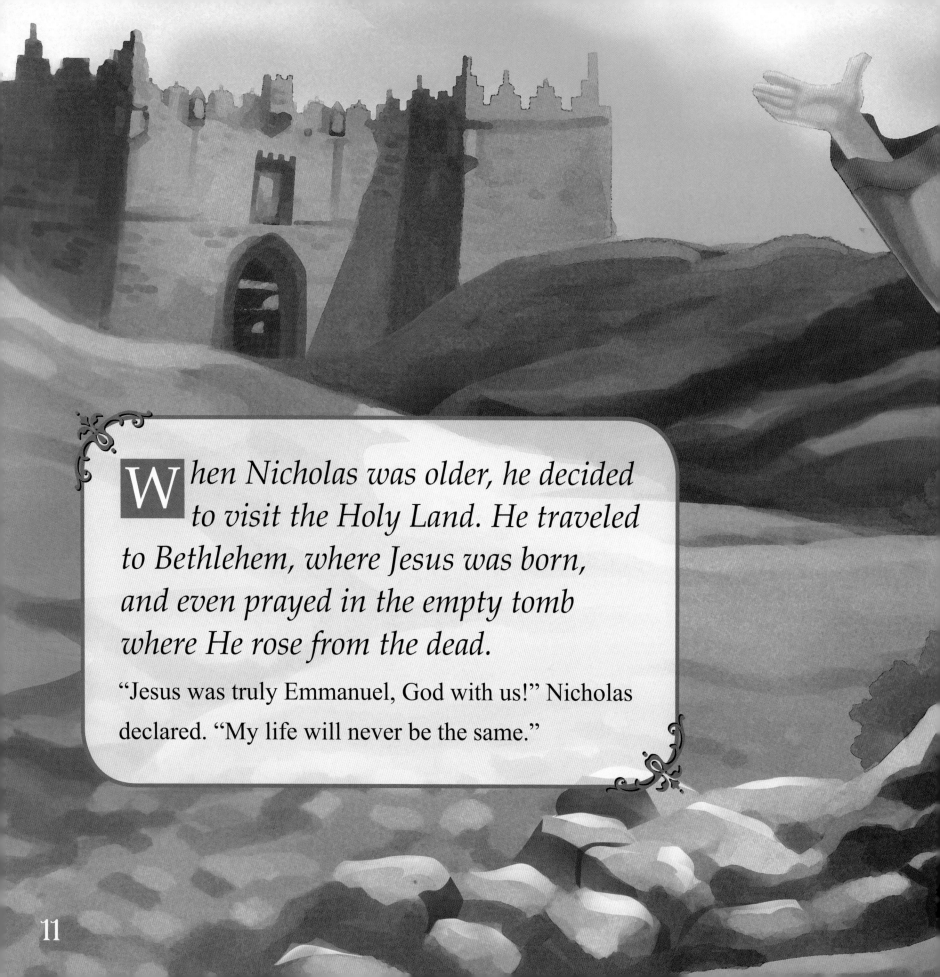

When Nicholas was older, he decided to visit the Holy Land. He traveled to Bethlehem, where Jesus was born, and even prayed in the empty tomb where He rose from the dead.

"Jesus was truly Emmanuel, God with us!" Nicholas declared. "My life will never be the same."

11

"My life will never be the same!"

S oon it was time for Nicholas to return to his homeland. He boarded the ship, and he and the crew began the long voyage to Lycia. One night the winds began to blow and the waves began to rage, rousing Nicholas from his deep sleep.

"I don't think we're going to make it to shore safely!" warned the captain.

Nicholas kneeled on the ship's deck, and as his body was tossed back and forth, he prayed, "Dear Jesus, please lead us to shore safely, and I promise I will give thanks to You upon our arrival on land." The waters calmed, and again the ship carried on her steady course for a city called Myra.

"Your prayers saved us!" cheered the crew.

"Dear Jesus, please lead us to shore safely, and I promise I will give thanks to You upon our arrival on land."

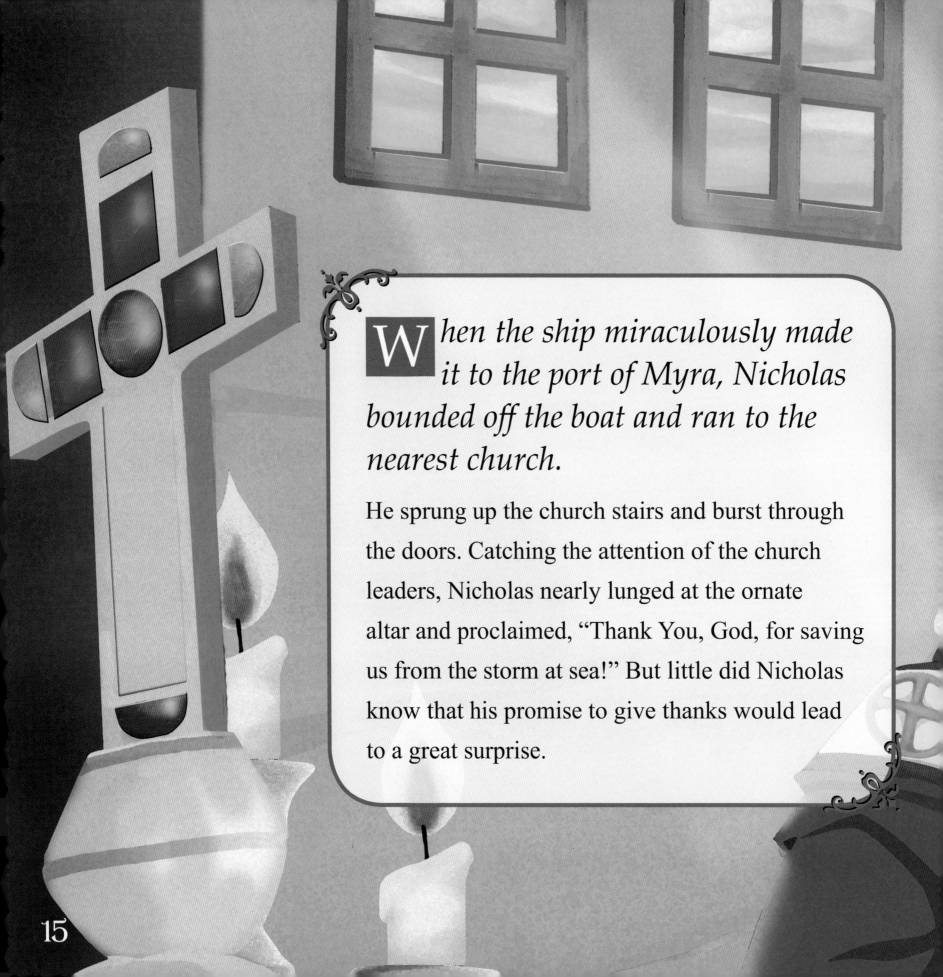

When the ship miraculously made it to the port of Myra, Nicholas bounded off the boat and ran to the nearest church.

He sprung up the church stairs and burst through the doors. Catching the attention of the church leaders, Nicholas nearly lunged at the ornate altar and proclaimed, "Thank You, God, for saving us from the storm at sea!" But little did Nicholas know that his promise to give thanks would lead to a great surprise.

The night before Nicholas' ship arrived, the church leaders could not agree who would be the next Bishop of Myra.

After arguing for some time, one of them said, "Let us have God choose the next leader. The first to walk through the doors of the church will be the bishop." Nicholas was that man. The men walked up to him, still kneeling, and said, "You are our new bishop!"

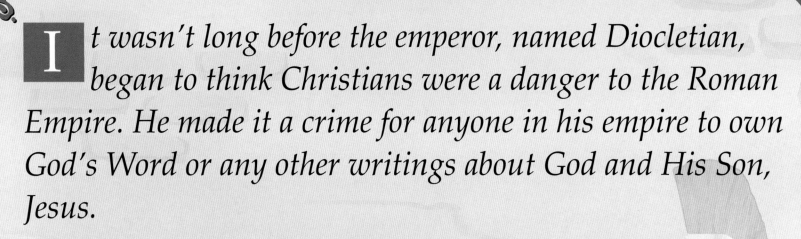

It wasn't long before the emperor, named Diocletian, began to think Christians were a danger to the Roman Empire. He made it a crime for anyone in his empire to own God's Word or any other writings about God and His Son, Jesus.

"To the fire!" the officials demanded when any Scriptures were found in homes. Many Christians sadly watched the Word of Life burn to ashes. Some were able to hide their copies, while others were sent to prison.

"To the fire!"

20

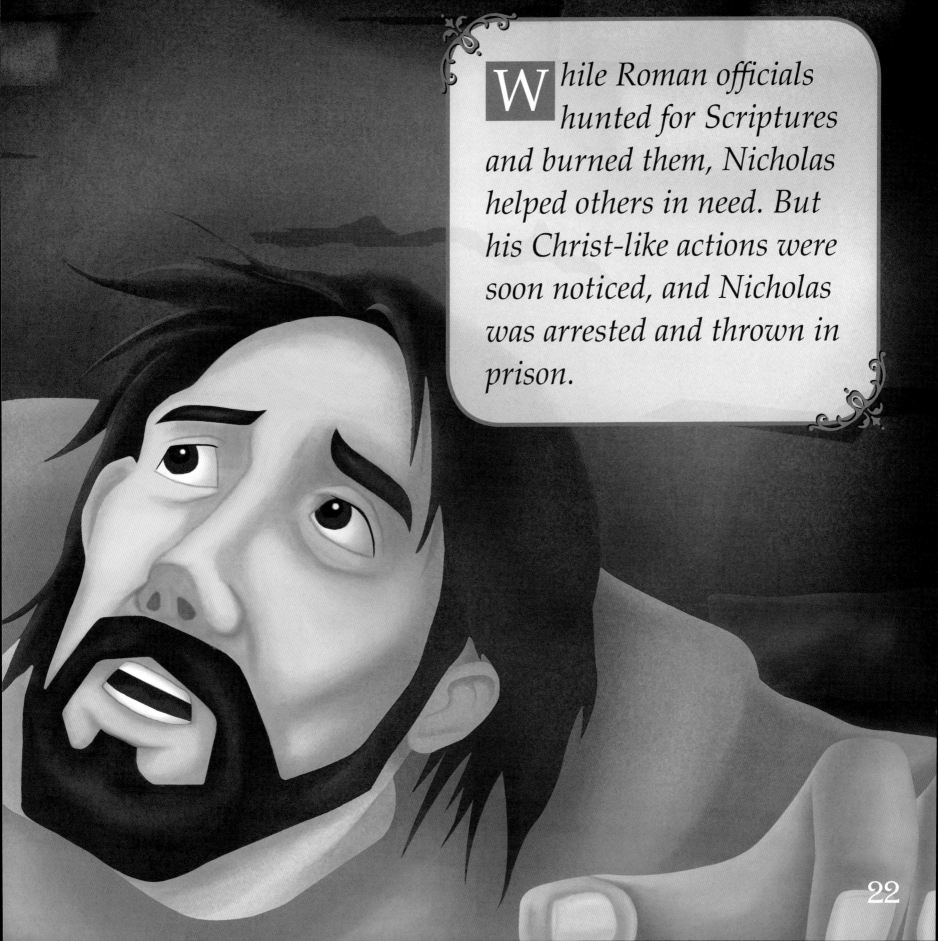

While Roman officials hunted for Scriptures and burned them, Nicholas helped others in need. But his Christ-like actions were soon noticed, and Nicholas was arrested and thrown in prison.

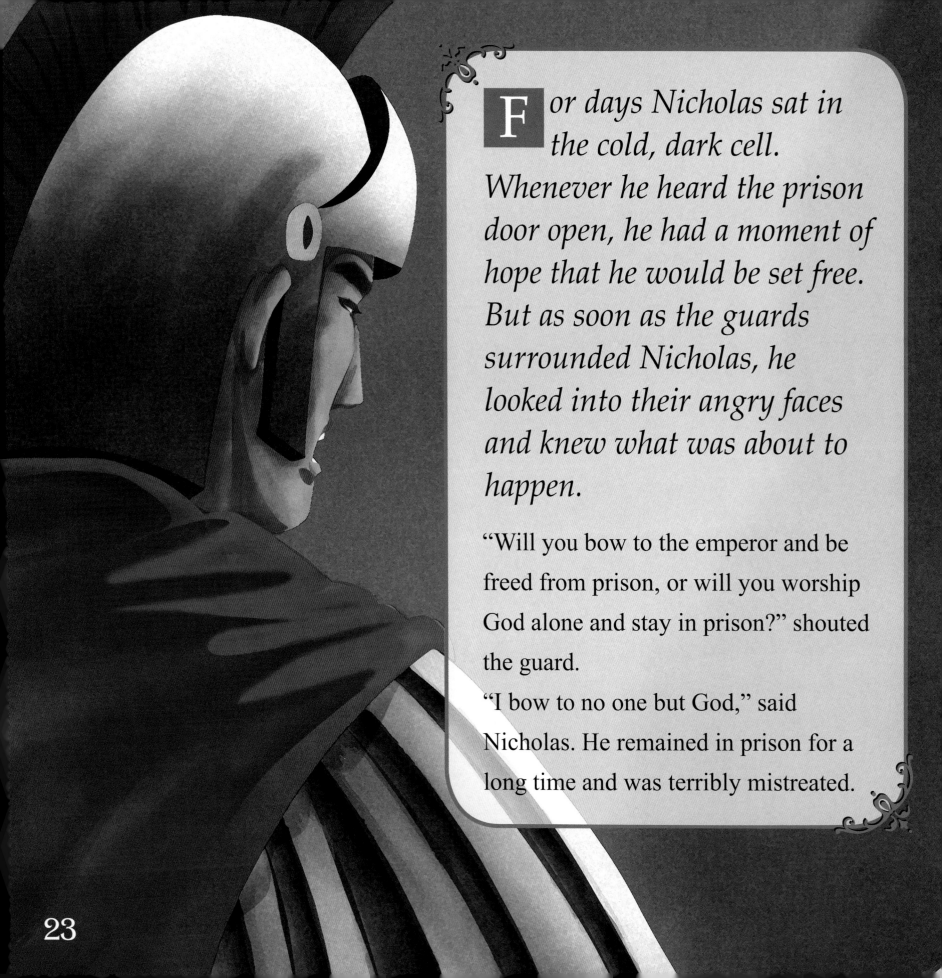

For days Nicholas sat in the cold, dark cell. Whenever he heard the prison door open, he had a moment of hope that he would be set free. But as soon as the guards surrounded Nicholas, he looked into their angry faces and knew what was about to happen.

"Will you bow to the emperor and be freed from prison, or will you worship God alone and stay in prison?" shouted the guard.

"I bow to no one but God," said Nicholas. He remained in prison for a long time and was terribly mistreated.

"Release all the Christians from prison!"

One day a new emperor took the throne. His name was Constantine, and he did not see the Christians as a danger to the Roman Empire. In fact, he believed the God of the Christians helped him win a battle to give him more control over the empire.

"Release all the Christians from prison!" ordered Constantine, and Nicholas was set free. But Nicholas' troubles were far from over.

A leader in the church named Arius taught that Jesus was created and had not existed with God since eternity past.

Those who followed Arius' teachings sang songs that made fun of God. The melodies were so catchy that people sang them on the streets on their way to school, at work and even at church.

A rius' teaching caused Christians to disagree about Jesus, so Emperor Constantine called a meeting of all the church leaders in the Roman Empire.

Tradition says that Arius and Nicholas were both at the meeting, and soon Arius began to sing his slanderous song. Furious that Arius would make fun of Jesus, Nicholas stood up and slapped him in the face. "How dare you shame our Lord!" shouted Nicholas.

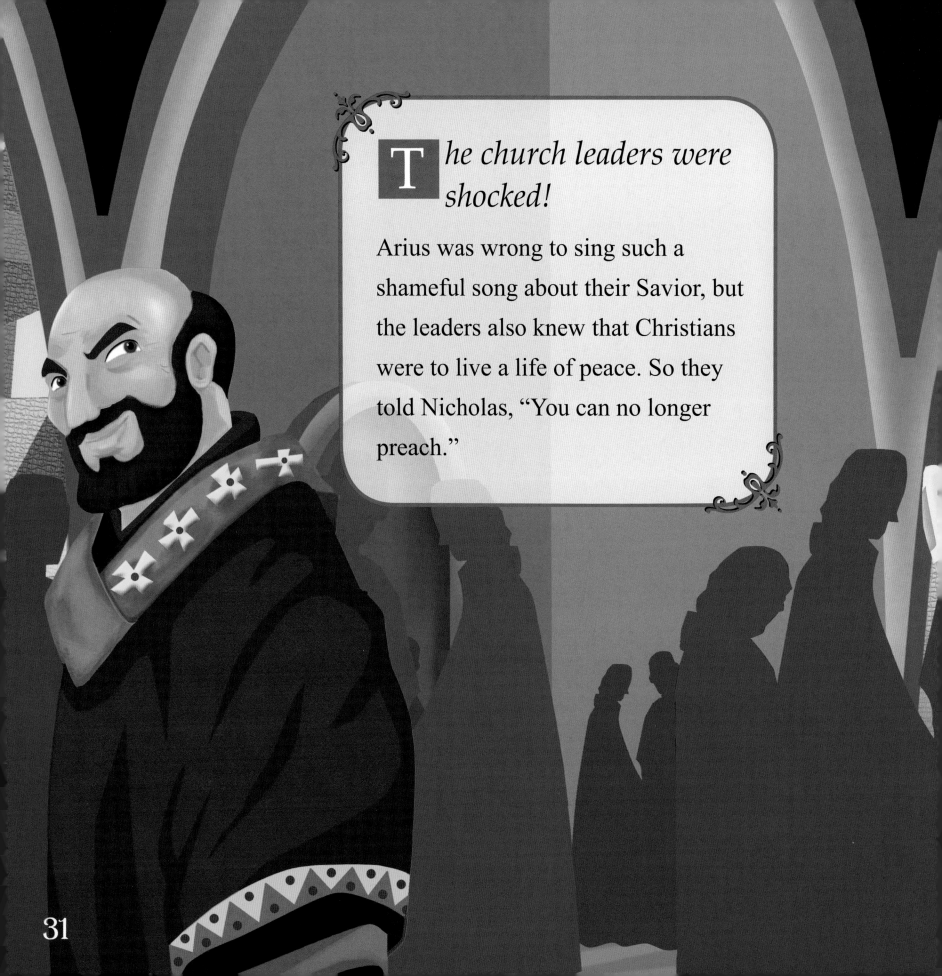

The church leaders were *shocked!*

Arius was wrong to sing such a shameful song about their Savior, but the leaders also knew that Christians were to live a life of peace. So they told Nicholas, "You can no longer preach."

"You can no longer preach."

32

Losing his job as bishop did not stop Nicholas from living alongside the poor, caring for the sick, and starting orphanages.

He continued to live out his generous heart until he died. Some believe he died in the year 343.

Hundreds of years have passed, and the life of Nicholas has lived on in legends that eventually brought us to the story of Santa Claus—a man with a white beard and a red suit who with his reindeer delivers presents to boys and girls on Christmas Eve.

In the Netherlands, he is known as Sinterklaas; and in Italy, Babbo Natale. But the story of Nicholas is one that we should remember. He suffered greatly for refusing to turn his back on Jesus Christ and stood up for Him when others made fun of Him.

T oday there are nations in the world where Christians are imprisoned as Nicholas was. In China, children are not allowed to learn about Jesus. And in Saudi Arabia, people are imprisoned if caught with a Bible.

Their courage to stand for Jesus despite imprisonment and rejection encourage us to live the same way and boldly tell others about Jesus, as Nicholas did.

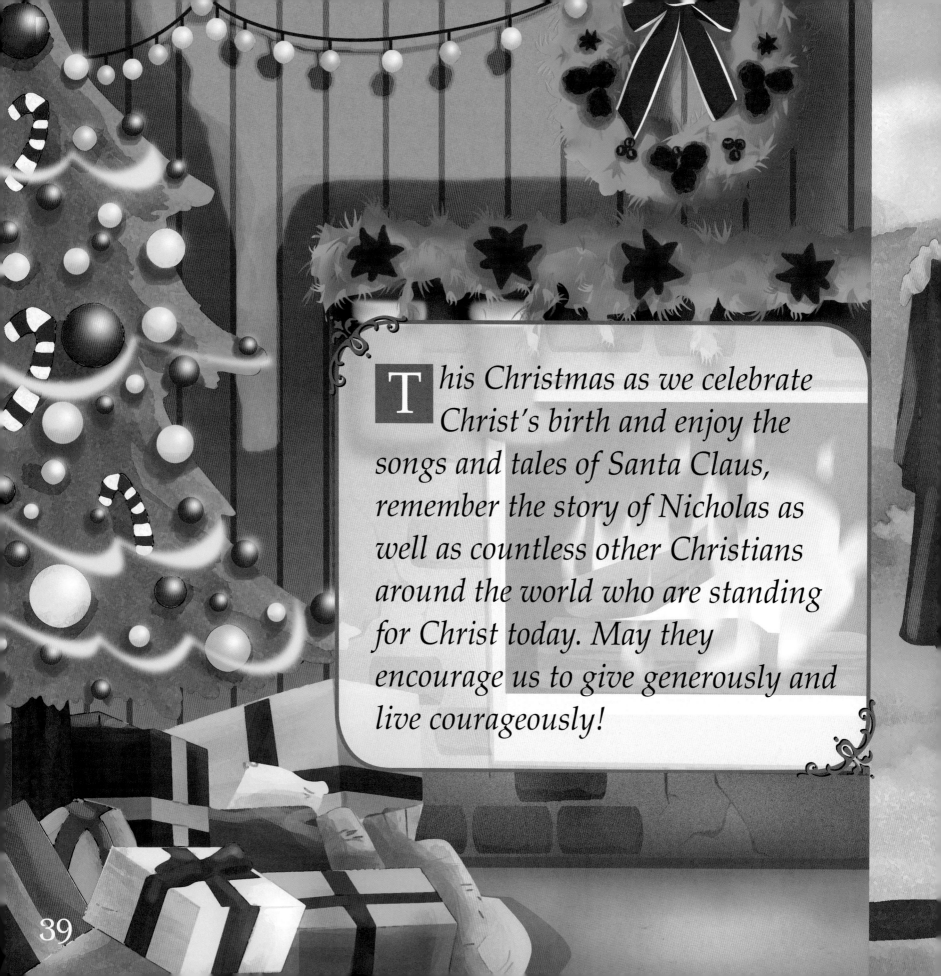

This Christmas as we celebrate Christ's birth and enjoy the songs and tales of Santa Claus, remember the story of Nicholas as well as countless other Christians around the world who are standing for Christ today. May they encourage us to give generously and live courageously!

For Reflection

"Yes, and all who desire to live godly in Christ Jesus will suffer persecution."
2 Timothy 3:12

What does it mean to live a godly life?
Why is one persecuted for living a godly life?
In what ways was Nicholas' life considered godly?
Why was Nicholas persecuted for being godly?
How can your life reflect God's character in your friendships, at school, and at home?

Prayer
Lord, thank You for the cloud of witnesses, like Nicholas, who have gone before us,
setting an example of faithfulness and godliness. Show me ways that my life can reflect
Your character, so that others may come to know You. Continue to strengthen and
encourage believers who live in nations that persecute them for telling others about You.
Amen.

Bibliography

Byfield, Ted (ed.) and Calvin Demmon (assoc. ed.). *The Christians Their First Two Thousand Years: By This Sign A.D. 250 to 350* (Canada: The Christian History Project, Inc., 2003).

Cowart, John W. *People Whose Faith Got Them Into Trouble* (Downers Grove, IL: InterVarsity Press, 1990).

González, Justo L. *The Early Church to the Dawn of the Reformation. Vol. 1 of The Story of Christianity.* (New York: HarperCollins, 1984).

Jöckle, Clemens. *Encyclopedia of Saints* (Old Saybrook, CT: Konecky & Konecky, 2003).

Maier, Paul. *Eusebius: The Church History* (Grand Rapids, MI: Kregel Publications, 1999).

"St. Nicholas." Catholic Online. Accessed on 20 January 2005. <http://www.catholic.org/saints/saint.php?saint_id=371 >.

"St. Nicholas of Myra." *The Catholic Encyclopedia, Volume XV*. Copyright © 1912 by Robert Appleton Company. Computer Edition Copyright © 2003 by Kevin Knight.

"Saint Nicholas of Myra Bishop, Confessor c. 342." Eternal Word Television Network. Accessed on 20 January 2005. <http://www.ewtn.com/library/MARY/NICHOLAS.htm>.

"Saints Who Loved the Blessed Sacrament: St. Nicholas of Bari {280-342}." Bulletin of the Eucharistic Crusade for Canada. <http://www.sspx.ca/EucharisticCrusade/2003_December/St_Nicholas_of_Bari.htm>.

Walsh, Michael (ed.). *Butler's Lives of Saints.* (San Francisco: Harper Collins, 1991), pp. 405-406.